Contents

Tour 1 - Map Vocabulary	2-3
Tour 2 - Pacific Region	4-5
Tour 3 - Southwest Region	6-7
Tour 4 - Mountain Region	8-9
Tour 5 - Western U.S. Review	10-11
Tour 6 - North Central Region	12-13
Tour 7 - Southeast Region	14-15
Tour 8 - Middle Atlantic and New England Regions	16-17
Tour 9 - North Central and Eastern U.S. Review	18-19
Tour 10 - United States	20-23
Tour 11 - U.S. Capitals	24-27
Tour 12 - Landforms	28-30
What I Learned	31
About the Author	32

Tour 1   Map Vocabulary

Label each item with its name.

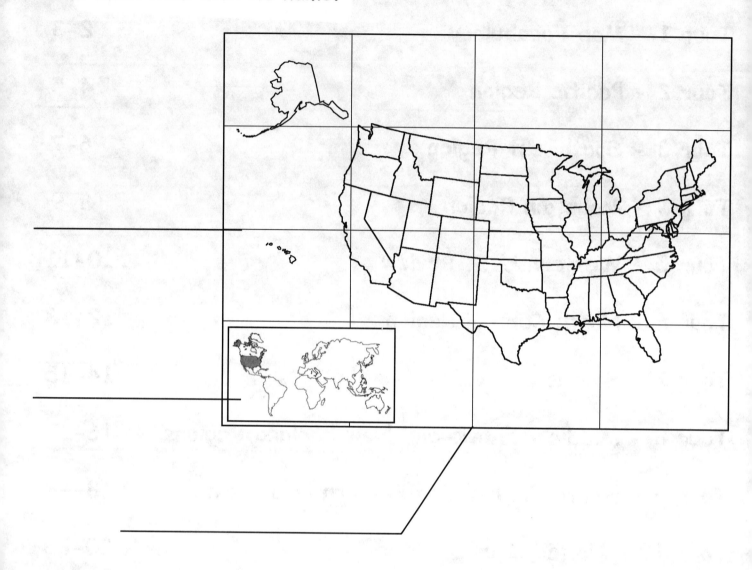

Compass Rose
Distance Scale
Inset Map
Lines of Latitude
Lines of Longitude
Map Key

Tour 1   Map Vocabulary

Compass Rose _____

_____

Distance Scale _____

_____

Inset Map _____

_____

Lines of Latitude _____

_____

Lines of Longitude _____

_____

Map Key _____

_____

Draw a compass rose.	Draw a distance scale.	Draw an inset map.
Draw lines of latitude.	Draw lines of longitude.	Draw a map key.

Tour 2 — Pacific Region

Label each state with its name.

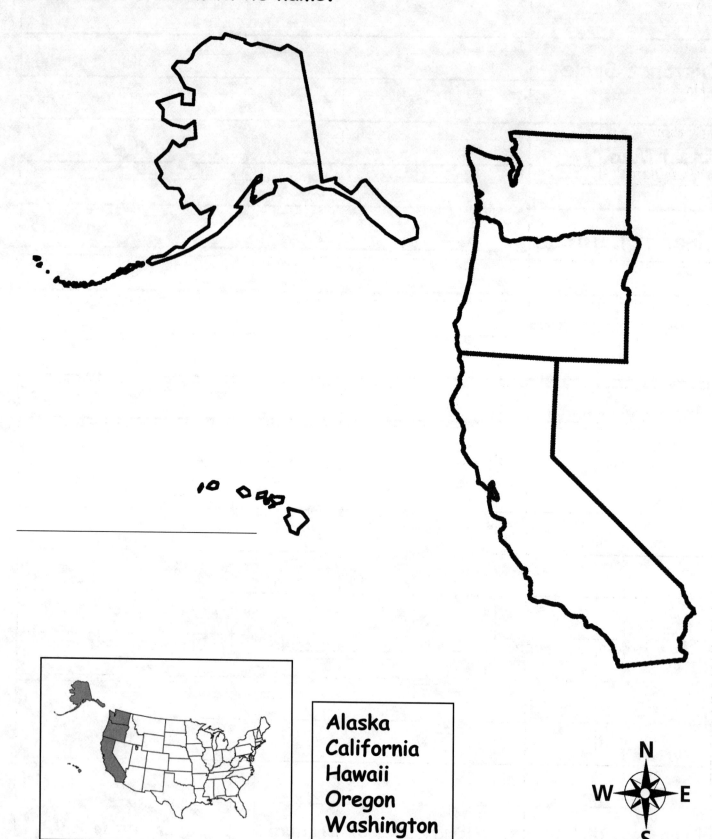

Alaska
California
Hawaii
Oregon
Washington

Tour 2　　　　　　　　　　Pacific Region

	Postal Abbr.	State Capital	State Nickname
Alaska			
California			
Hawaii			
Oregon			
Washington			

My GeoJourney Journal

_____
_____
_____
_____
_____
_____
_____
_____
_____
_____
_____
_____
_____
_____

Tour 3   Southwest Region

Label each state with its name.

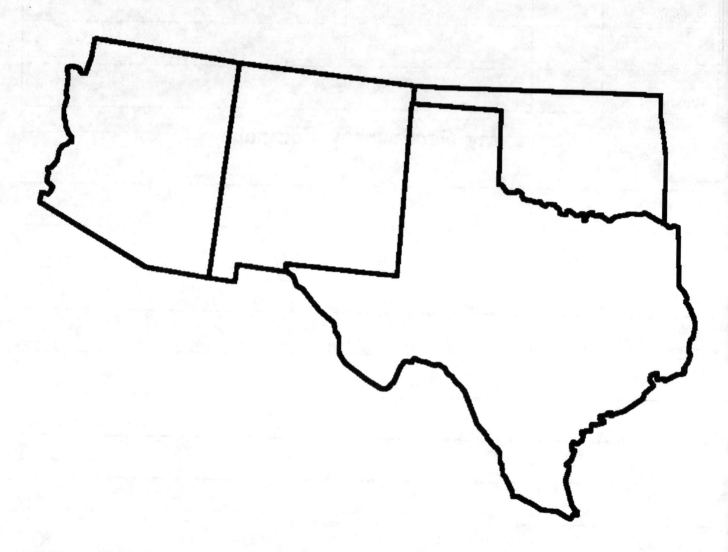

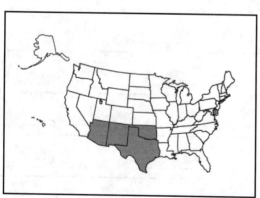

Arizona
New Mexico
Oklahoma
Texas

Tour 3　　　　　　　Southwest Region

	Postal Abbr.	State Capital	State Nickname
Arizona			
New Mexico			
Oklahoma			
Texas			

My GeoJourney Journal

_____
_____
_____
_____
_____
_____
_____
_____
_____
_____
_____
_____
_____
_____
_____

Tour 4 — Mountain Region

Label each state with its name.

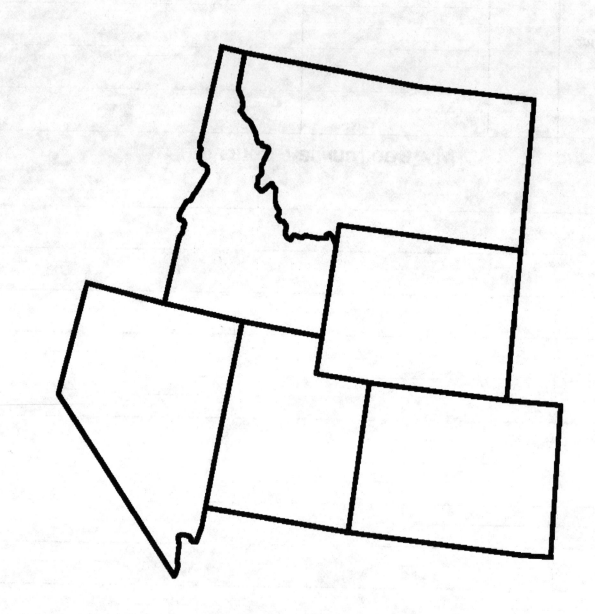

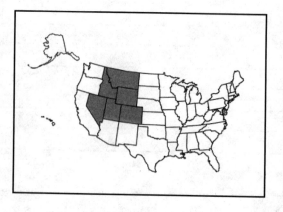

Colorado
Idaho
Montana
Nevada
Utah
Wyoming

Tour 4 — Mountain Region

	Postal Abbr.	State Capital	State Nickname
Colorado			
Idaho			
Montana			
Nevada			
Utah			
Wyoming			

My GeoJourney Journal

_____
_____
_____
_____
_____
_____
_____
_____
_____
_____
_____
_____
_____

Tour 5 — Western U.S. Review

Label each state with its postal abbreviation.

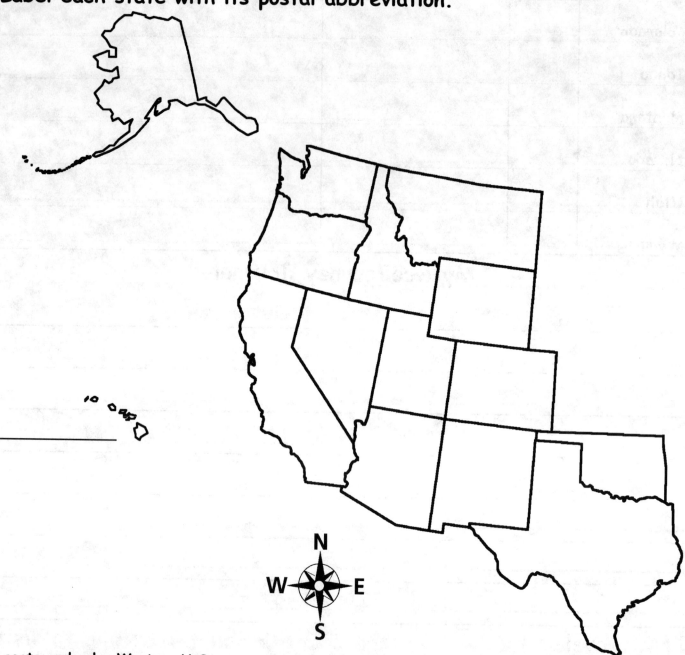

Locate and color Western U.S. Review States.

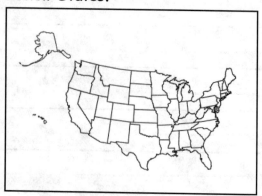

Alaska (AK)
Arizona (AZ)
California (CA)
Colorado (CO)
Hawaii (HI)
Idaho (ID)
Montana (MT)
Nevada (NV)
New Mexico (NM)
Oklahoma (OK)
Oregon (OR)
Texas (TX)
Utah (UT)
Washington (WA)
Wyoming (WY)

Tour 5 Western U.S. Review

Land and Water

_____
_____
_____
_____
_____
_____
_____

Crops and Natural Resources

_____
_____
_____
_____
_____
_____

If I traveled to the Western U.S., I would most like to visit the state of _____

because _____
_____
_____

Tour 6 — North Central Region

Label each state with its name.

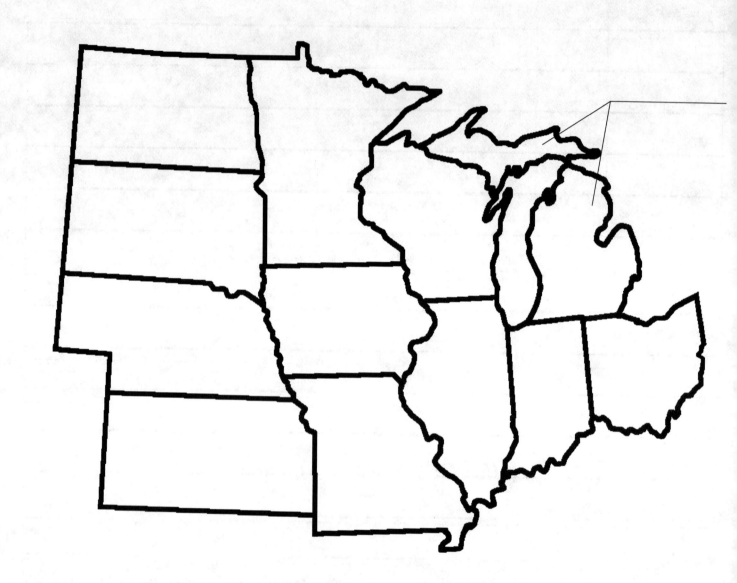

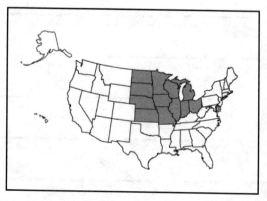

Illinois	Missouri
Indiana	Nebraska
Iowa	North Dakota
Kansas	Ohio
Michigan	South Dakota
Minnesota	Wisconsin

Tour 6 — North Central Region

	Postal Abbr.	State Capital	State Nickname
Illinois			
Indiana			
Iowa			
Kansas			
Michigan			
Minnesota			
Missouri			
Nebraska			
North Dakota			
Ohio			
South Dakota			
Wisconsin			

My GeoJourney Journal

_____
_____
_____
_____
_____
_____
_____

Tour 7   Southeast Region

Label each state with its name.

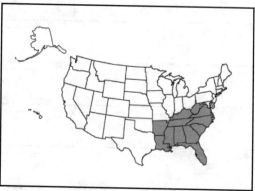

Alabama	Mississippi
Arkansas	North Carolina
Florida	South Carolina
Georgia	Tennessee
Kentucky	Virginia
Louisiana	West Virginia

Tour 7　　　　　　　　Southeast Region

	Postal Abbr.	State Capital	State Nickname
Alabama			
Arkansas			
Florida			
Georgia			
Kentucky			
Louisiana			
Mississippi			
North Carolina			
South Carolina			
Tennessee			
Virginia			
West Virginia			

My GeoJourney Journal

_____
_____
_____
_____
_____
_____
_____

Tour 8 — Middle Atlantic & New England Regions

Label each state with its name.

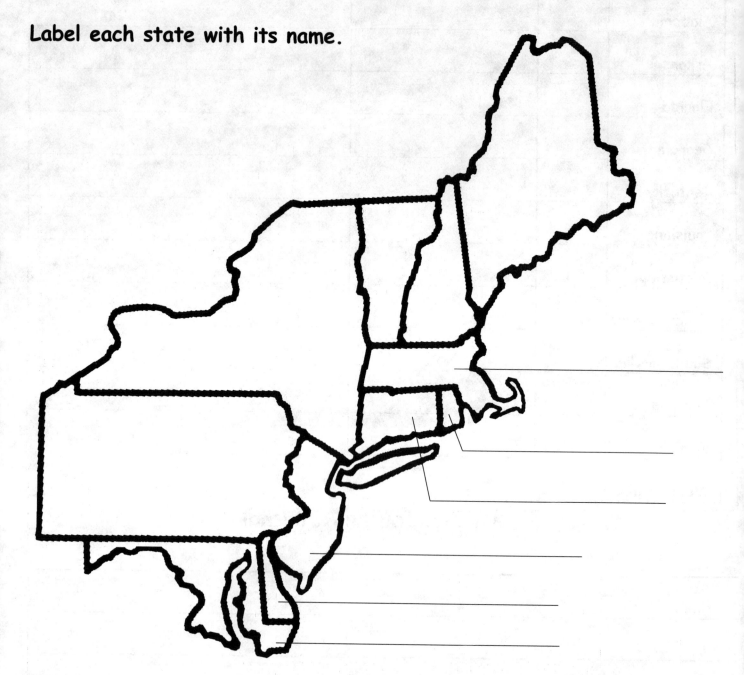

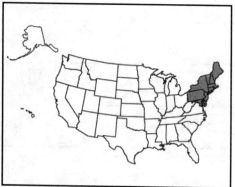

Connecticut	New Jersey
Delaware	New York
Maine	Pennsylvania
Maryland	Rhode Island
Massachusetts	Vermont
New Hampshire	

Tour 8   Middle Atlantic & New England Regions

	Postal Abbr.	State Capital	State Nickname
Connecticut			
Delaware			
Maine			
Maryland			
Massachusetts			
New Hampshire			
New Jersey			
New York			
Pennsylvania			
Rhode Island			
Vermont			

My GeoJourney Journal

_____

_____

_____

_____

_____

_____

_____

Tour 9 North Central and Eastern U.S. Review

Label each state with its postal abbreviation.

Locate and color North Central and Eastern U.S. Review States.

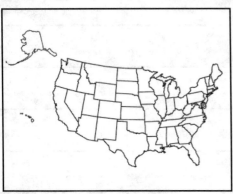

Alabama (AL)	Maryland (MD)	Pennsylvania (PA)
Arkansas (AR)	Massachusetts (MA)	Rhode Island (RI)
Connecticut (CT)	Michigan (MI)	South Carolina (SC)
Delaware (DE)	Minnesota (MN)	South Dakota (SD)
Florida (FL)	Mississippi (MS)	Tennessee (TN)
Georgia (GA)	Missouri (MO)	Vermont (VT)
Illinois (IL)	Nebraska (NE)	Virginia (VA)
Indiana (IN)	New Hampshire (NH)	West Virginia (WV)
Iowa (IA)	New Jersey (NJ)	Wisconsin (WI)
Kansas (KS)	New York (NY)	
Kentucky (KY)	North Carolina (NC)	
Louisiana (LA)	North Dakota (ND)	
Maine (ME)	Ohio (OH)	

Tour 9 North Central and Eastern U.S. Review

Land and Water

_____
_____
_____
_____
_____
_____
_____

Crops and Natural Resources

_____
_____
_____
_____
_____
_____

If I traveled to the Eastern U.S., I would most like to visit the state of _____

because _____
_____
_____

Tour 10

United States

Alabama (AL)
Alaska (AK)
Arizona (AZ)
Arkansas (AR)
California (CA)
Colorado (CO)
Connecticut (CT)
Delaware (DE)
Florida (FL)
Georgia (GA)
Hawaii (HI)
Idaho (ID)
Illinois (IL)
Indiana (IN)
Iowa (IA)
Kansas (KS)
Kentucky (KY)

Louisiana (LA)
Maine (ME)
Maryland (MD)
Massachusetts (MA)
Michigan (MI)
Minnesota (MN)
Mississippi (MS)
Missouri (MO)
Montana (MT)
Nebraska (NE)
Nevada (NV)
New Hampshire (NH)
New Jersey (NJ)
New Mexico (NM)
New York (NY)
North Carolina (NC)
North Dakota (ND)

Ohio (OH)
Oklahoma (OK)
Oregon (OR)
Pennsylvania (PA)
Rhode Island (RI)
South Carolina (SC)
South Dakota (SD)
Tennessee (TN)
Texas (TX)
Utah (UT)
Vermont (VT)
Virginia (VA)
Washington (WA)
West Virginia (WV)
Wisconsin (WI)
Wyoming (WY)

Tour 10

Label each state with its correct postal abbreviation, which is found on the previous page.

United States

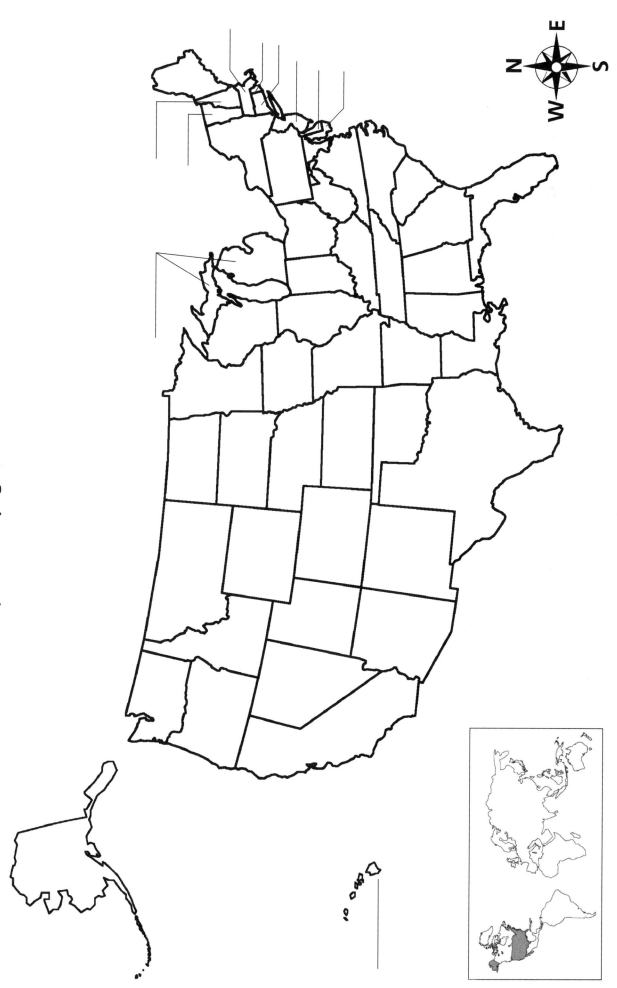

21

Tour 10   United States

Interesting Historical Facts about the U.S.

_____
_____
_____
_____
_____
_____
_____

I live in _____. It is
                     (my home state)

located in the _____ region

of the United States.

Interesting Historical Facts about My State

_____
_____
_____
_____
_____
_____
_____

Tour 10 United States

Interesting Natural Attractions of the U.S.

_____
_____
_____
_____
_____
_____
_____
_____
_____

Interesting Man-Made Attractions in the U.S.

_____
_____
_____
_____
_____
_____
_____
_____
_____

Tour 11
U.S. Capitals

On the following page, place the correct postal abbreviation on the line beside its state capital.

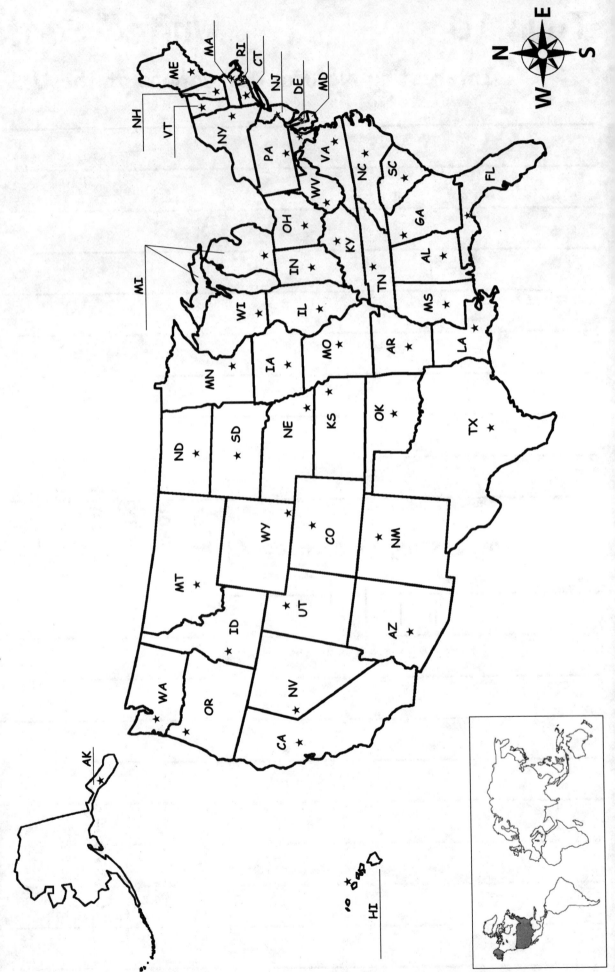

Tour 11

U.S. Capitals

___ Albany
___ Annapolis
___ Atlanta
___ Augusta
___ Austin
___ Baton Rouge
___ Bismarck
___ Boise
___ Boston
___ Carson City
___ Charleston
___ Cheyenne
___ Columbia
___ Columbus
___ Concord
___ Denver
___ Des Moines

___ Dover
___ Frankfort
___ Harrisburg
___ Hartford
___ Helena
___ Honolulu
___ Indianapolis
___ Jackson
___ Jefferson City
___ Juneau
___ Lansing
___ Lincoln
___ Little Rock
___ Madison
___ Montgomery
___ Montpelier
___ Nashville

___ Oklahoma City
___ Olympia
___ Phoenix
___ Pierre
___ Providence
___ Raleigh
___ Richmond
___ Sacramento
___ Salem
___ Salt Lake City
___ Santa Fe
___ Springfield
___ St. Paul
___ Tallahassee
___ Topeka
___ Trenton

Tour 11   U.S. Capitals
My GeoJourney Journal

_____
_____
_____
_____
_____
_____
_____
_____
_____
_____

If I traveled to any U.S. capital city, I would most like to visit the city of _____

because _____
_____
_____
_____
_____
_____

Tour 11   U.S. Capitals

My state's capital city is _____.
It is located in the U.S. state of _____,
and it is in the _____ region of the country.

My GeoJourney Journal

_____
_____
_____
_____
_____
_____
_____
_____
_____
_____
_____
_____
_____
_____
_____

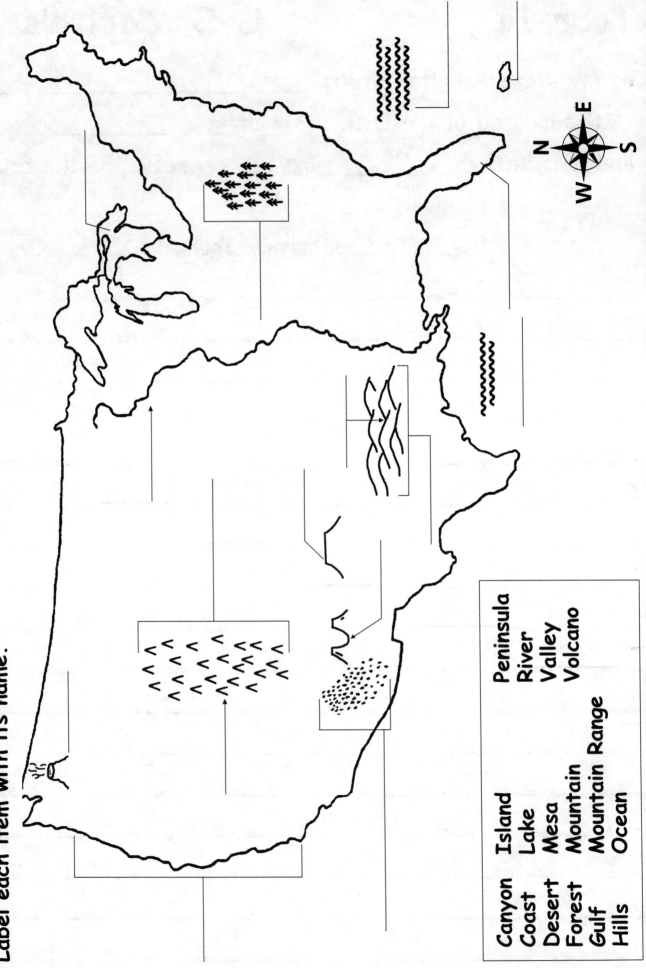

Tour 12   Landforms

Write information about 10 landforms.

1. _____

_____

2. _____

_____

3. _____

_____

4. _____

_____

5. _____

_____

6. _____

_____

7. _____

_____

8. _____

_____

9. _____

_____

10. _____

_____

Tour 12   Landforms

Some of the landforms and natural resources in the area where I live are _____
_____
_____
_____
_____
_____

Where I live, people have these kinds of jobs because of the landforms and natural resources.

_____
_____
_____
_____
_____
_____

The climate (weather) in the area where I live is _____
_____
_____

My GeoJourney

During my GeoJourney adventure, I learned _____

_____

_____

_____

_____

_____

_____

_____

_____

Final GeoJourney thoughts: _____

_____

_____

_____

_____

_____

_____

_____

About the Author

My full name is _____.

I was born in _____.

My birthday is _____.

I am _____ years old. I am in the _____ grade.

My teacher's name is _____.

I live with _____
_____.

When I grow up I would like to be a _____
because _____
_____.

More about me _____
_____
_____
_____